How to Give up Drinking

and be part of the world again

Francesca Hepton

ISBN: 978-1-9999126-7-3

OWN IT

HATE IT

BEAT IT

CONTENTS

Also by Francesca Hepton
*in the **How to...** series:*

Look Young and be more grateful, grounded and gorgeous
Be Happy
Stop Smoking and Start Living
Get Fit with Reiki and Music
Save Money

First published in 2017
by Babili Books
a division of Babili Services Ltd
UK company

INTRODUCTION

LET'S BE CLEAR

Who this book is written for:

Mothers who are multi-tasking trying to keep a picture-magazine-perfect house, being a successful, busy entrepreneur, coming home at late hours and reaching for "mummy's little helper": that smooth glass of red wine that will take them into a state of "oblivion" [1] and help them forget the stresses of the day.

Recognise yourself?

Or is this you:

Women from managerial and professional socio-economic groups - aka 'high fliers' - also drink heavily on a regular basis.

(And as an interesting side note, women in manual occupations tend to drink less alcohol over a week than their "blue-collar" counterparts. [2])

---

[1] "Oblivion Drinker" by Antonia Hoyle, Daily Mail 2013
[2] Institute of Alcohol Studies: Women and alcohol Factsheet - Updated May 2013

Other characteristics you may recognise:

Drinking at home, sometimes even alone if you are divorced or separated.

But largely, this guide is for women between the age of 35 and 45 who have isolated themselves from their own lives through drinking.

Of course these parameters are not static. If you are 46 it does not mean you should put this book down or that it won't be useful for you. My ball-part figure is meant to denote "middle-aged" women – but middle-aged always sounds so twee and even older than 45!

Even though there is a large number of women over 45 who are heavy drinkers, recent figures show it is middle-class professional women (aged 45-64) who are now drinking the most. The report by the Organisation for Economic Co-Operation and Development reveals that women in the UK are twice as likely to be problem drinkers if they have a good education, (Anna Moore, Daily Mail) – quite surprising. I want to help you stop before it is too late.

I want to help you before you get to the "Empty nest syndrome" - women aged 45 to 60+ represent a segment of society that is drinking even more dangerous levels. If you can get your life on track, feel a sense of purpose and worth for yourself as a woman, not as a mother, before your children leave home, then you are set to avoid that feeling of further sadness and loss when your children actually do fly the nest.

The difficulties for women in this older age group is that they are also more likely to have parents who no longer support them, but instead require their help. Elderly parents can place heavy demands on their daughters who are already juggling busy jobs, running a home and raising teenage children.

You need to be fit and energised to cope with all this. Not to mention the sadness of when your parents eventually come to pass away, adding even more pressure onto you.

Start looking after yourself now and you will not see your parents as a burden. You will not regret your children leaving home. It will not be too late for you to fulfil the dreams and aspirations you had as a young woman. If you continue to mistreat your body and mind, you will not have the energy and focus to deal with your own life, let alone be able to help those you love.

I must point out that I am not being sexist when I say that "daughters" are the ones to look after their parents. Just as it is the women who tend to do the housework more than the men or look after the children more than the men, it is the women who tend to look after the parents.

Whether it's nurturing a baby, looking after an ill sibling or caring for an older adult, women have always been at the forefront of caregiving. Despite the trend towards a more gender-balanced family caregiver population, 2012 figures from the U.S. National Alliance for Caregiving still have the proportion of female family caregivers in the majority; at 66 per cent (AgingCare.com, 2016).

Trying to find that balance between looking after your own family and being a carer for your parents can be at the sacrifice of your own aspirations, both professional and personal. Drinking will not help you with this delicate balancing act. It will only hamper your efforts, in more ways than you think. You will be less able to offer help because you are not well yourself.

As we have all heard over the years, but perhaps chosen to ignore, alcohol affects women more than men. Women have fewer of the enzymes needed to break down alcohol, meaning we feel the effects of drinking to a greater degree and quicker. Not only do we hit that state of "drunkenness" with less drink, our livers are also more susceptible to fail – not a reassuring fact! Perhaps if you could see yours, you would stop drinking. Or if you pondered on your increased chances of getting mouth, bowl, oesophagus or breast cancer with every sip you take, you would not go for a second third or fourth glass.

The effects on the brain.

Mental health is an invisible problem. It is an area women ought to give more thought to, as they are twice as likely to suffer from anxiety, depression and the effects of stress than men.

And this trend is not showing any signs of slowing. For women in high-pressure job such as chief executives, doctors and lawyers, the number of deaths caused by drinking has risen by 23%.

And at lower management level, those losing their lives to liver disease and other conditions caused by alcohol rose from 247 to 290 – a 17% hike. [2]

You are even making the headlines girls. For the past decade now, but not for the right reasons:

"Women aged 40 to 50 are the fastest growing group of dependent drinkers." (Express, 2017)

The trend is also a global one. It is not isolated to the UK or the USA or other European countries:

More than 500,000 middle-aged Australian women are engaging in high-risk drinking and there is insufficient help available, researchers have warned.

Dubbed the "sandwich generation", researchers described a cohort of women aged 35 to 59 drowning under the pressures of teenage children, ageing parents, work responsibilities and demanding partners.

You are not alone.

Definition of dependent

Dependence is not just a habit or psychological phenomena; it is also a biological and physical manifestation of our genetics and biological make-up:

Advancements in neurobiological research have changed the way we view *addiction*. *Addiction* is no longer limited to problematic substance use. We now know that certain activities can also be *addictive* (e.g. sex, gambling). This is because addiction is a problem of brain functioning. We become *addicted* to the chemicals our brain releases, not the substance or activity that causes this release. Our genetics greatly determine our brain functioning. (AMHC)

This suggests that it is the make-up of our brain rather than our lack of willpower that makes us take up the habit of drinking. In addition to this, the more you "poison" your brain with alcohol, the less capable you are of making the right decision. The brain is a very powerful tool though, it will get one message across clear and strong: Keep drinking it is pleasurable.

And because it does give off this message, you compulsively and repeatedly go on drinking and even after giving up, you are likely to relapse – that is if you have not re-trained your brain (See Step 3 and the final chapter on Relapse).

As if you needed convincing even more, I want to explain to you how our biological (female) make-up influences our drinking habits and what the resulting affects are:

Higher blood ethanol concentrations can affect the risk of dependence at an earlier stage for women. *Dependence* jumps dramatically for men who exceed 7/8 drinks per occasion, but it can affect women sooner, i.e. women who drink 5/6 drinks per occasion (aka binge drinking levels - Institute of Alcohol Studies).

Heavy steady chronic drinking at sufficiently high levels can also lead to the physiological changes that result in alcohol *dependence* – including liver disease such as cirrhosis and hepatitis – after a comparatively shorter period of heavy consumption than men."[3]

Some women are at high-risk of their drinking leading to *dependence*. Because of their diminished ability to deal with stress (as a result of drinking), they are more likely to drink if they have the urge.

Perhaps you can empathise with that sentiment? Life and problems getting harder and harder to stay on top of. Alcohol helps you "cope" with the stress you are experiencing in everyday life compounded with bad experiences or traumas you have suffered (losing someone you love, divorce, job loss, etc.).

Not sure what I mean?

Take a look around in society. Have you not noticed how hard it is to judge a woman's true age? The glitzy stars on our screens are making young boys swoon even when the ladies are in their 40s and 50s – look at Angelina Joline, Jennifer Aniston, Michelle Pfeiffer, Elizabeth Hurley, Sharon Stone, Madonna – sorry if you are gorgeous and I haven't mentioned you! There is so much pressure to look perfect.

It's not just the Botox and hair dye. Girls are sculpting themselves. Some of this is positive as they are looking after their bodies and their minds. Getting into yoga, pilates, meditation. Feeding their inner selves as well as their outward appearance.

We are entering the realms of agelessness. A 20-year old girl could easily be mistaken for a 40-year old woman and vice-versa.

The fact that young girls always want to look older than their years also contributes to this growing trend. In fact, in my personal opinion, young girls under the age of 20, as girls have down since time immemorial, are

---

[3] Institute of Alcohol Studies: Women and alcohol Factsheet - Updated May 2013

applying far too much make-up in the form of foundation and false lashes, in their effort to look more mature. When by contrast, if they were to let their fresh young skin breath not only would they stop the aging affect of the make-up, they would allow their naturally radiant, supple and toned skin shine through. Something which is much more appealing and something which the older ladies are trying to emulate through foundation. It is a nonsensical vicious cycle. (See my book: How to look young).

The main reason I am bringing up these forced efforts of young girls to grow up, is to show through this example, how we as women feel we have to be something that we are not. We force ourselves to be everything right from a young age.

We say to the world:

"Look at me, not only am I **beautiful**, not only am I **fit** but I am also very **successful** in my work/studies." We compete constantly with men at the level of work and sports, but on top of this we are also striving to be that perfect sexy goddess all men desire. It becomes even more of a strain as we then have to fit in the role of motherhood.

"Look world, I can juggle being gorgeous, a great cook, the best mother, have the cleanest house and be a successful business woman."

What the hell!!??!!

Why do we do this to ourselves? You don't see men struggling to keep the kitchen spotless whilst fighting cellulite on their behinds and taking lessons in how to learn Spanish and reading up on how to best deal with teenage kids! No, they have a much more laid-back and pragmatic realistic approach: "I go to work, I meet with the guys, love my kids, go to the gym when I want, love my wife no matter what she is wearing." You get the idea of the "clichéd" picture.

Put yourself first for a change, it will help others.

Are your male partners really being selfish?

If you look after yourself, you have more to give others. You are not tied up in knots of worry and anxiety and depression. You can give off positivity instead of resentment and regret.

Take the analogy of inflight safety procedures on an airplane.

Put the mask over yourself first then help your children.

Men don't have a problem with this – if you were to put the mask on your child, but they were fussing or something went wrong, you then could not help them because you would not be able to. Put the oxygen mask on you first, be prepared, look after yourself. Then you can help your children or those who need your help without fear of running out of time; you can deal with the situation by looking after yourself first.

Women seem to naturally put the weight of the world on their shoulders and of course at some stage your shoulders cannot take the strain anymore on their own. Instead of admitting that you need help, you reach out for a different kind of crutch. One that will lift you and make you feel better, more relaxed and more confident.

This, ladies, is where you, like I, turned to that fickle friend called alcohol. Promising everything through droopy rose-tinted glasses, at first you feel it is helping you get through the days.

The joys of a wee drinky-poo!

Alcohol helps you get through the day knowing that when you finally come home and kick off your heels (metaphorically speaking), you can enjoy a glass of wine and unwind. Ridding yourself of the stresses and strains of the day you feel yourself melt into a warm and hazy sense of floating euphoria. At parties or social gatherings, you are able to muster some of that inner sparkle that you really did not think you had left in you after a gruelling week with the kids and work, but thanks to your friend alcohol, you manage to smile and shine and laugh with your friends.

This alleged friend of yours does not come alone though. He has a friend of his own. Mr Hangover and he can be a real killer sometimes. Mr Hangover ruins your entire day. Making you shout at the children and your partner, making you unfocussed at work. Making you forgetful. And Mr Hangover also comes with a friend, too. He is called Mr Depletion. Mr Depletion literally depletes your body of all its energy resources because you can no longer absorb the nutrients your body needs.

Alcohol use inhibits absorption of nutrients. Not only is alcohol itself devoid of proteins, minerals, and vitamins, it actually inhibits the absorption and usage of vital nutrients such as thiamine (vitamin B1), vitamin B12, folic acid, and zinc. What do you need these vitamins and minerals for?

Thiamine helps with the metabolism of proteins and fat and the formation of haemoglobin. It is also essential for optimising your physical performance through its role in metabolizing carbohydrates.

Vitamin B12 is essential for your good health. It helps maintain healthy red blood and nerve cells.

Folic acid is an integral part of a coenzyme involved in the formation of new cells; low levels of folic acid can lead to a blood disorder called "megaloblastic anemia", which causes a lowering of your body's capacity to carry oxygen. [4]

I think you get picture: By drinking high levels of alcohol, **you are starving your body of essential nutrients.**

---

[4] Student Health Services, Accredited by Accreditation Association for Amulatory Health Care, Inc.

Ready to start the journey of how to say goodbye to Mr Hangover and Mr Depletion?

It's as easy as 1, 2, 3. Own it – Hate – Beat it!

Step 1

OWN IT

Acknowledge your problem and do something about it

Change of routine

The "change" has to be sustainable not a quick-fix.

You need to reach out to your family and friends for support. There are support groups as well who will help you keep on track.

Do not wait for a crisis to change your habit. You need to decide your own turning point. Do not wait until you are dying of liver failure or have smashed up your car or run someone over drink driving or deprived your children of their basic essentials so that you can fund your habit.

You need to say STOP to yourself NOW. You need to decide your turning point is today.

I remember the day I changed my routine. It was the day I kicked my parasite of a partner out of the house. When I kicked him out, I kicked out all the other things in my life that were sucking my life force out of me. Just like he was draining me, so were all my bad habits. It was such a relief to not have to drink any more.

I associated my drinking with my pathetic degenerate relationship. What do you associate your drinking habit with? A job you hate? The way you look? A failed career? A failed marriage? Disobedient teenage kids? A hurtful experience in your past?

Whatever you associate or even "blame" your dependency on, you need to face that problem. Hone in on it and understand truly if that is your reason or rather your excuse for drinking. If you can do this then that is the element of your life you need to "rectify". It may not be as simple as I make it sound. I was able to physically kick my problem out. Emotions and hurt cannot be physically removed from your life. All the torment and torture that I endured in my relationship did not leave when his physical presence left my home and my life, but what did happen was that I was able to be myself. I was not living under his shadow. If you are able, you need to remove whoever or whatever is shadowing you out. Find yourself. Be yourself. I guarantee that that version of you does not want to be dependent on drink.

The true version of you wants to live and feel free and happy again.

I refer again to this "true" version of yourself in Step 3. It is essential that you be true to yourself in order to:

1.   OWN YOUR DEPENDENCY

2.   HATE YOUR DEPENDENCY

3.   BEAT YOUR DEPENDENCY

If you miss out Step 1 and do not even admit to yourself that you are dependent on alcohol, you cannot begin this journey. It all starts with being honest with yourself. You cannot feel shame in front of yourself. You alone know why you are drinking and why you think you cannot stop. Do not feel ashamed, feel decisive instead.

You can stop. You can gain control. You need to be open with yourself and say: "I want to stop drinking" and then understand what is the factor or influence or failure that you believe is causing you to continue to drink. Some may say it is just habit. Well that is easily remedied – further on in this chapter we have some schedules for you to follow to start up a new routine with new "good" habits to replace the old "bad" habits. Retraining your brain will be child's play.

If, on the other hand there is a deep-rooted reason for your dependency, going beyond mere habit, you need to be that much braver and face it.

My reason for drinking left by the front door as my partner walked out of my life, and I was able to change my habits instantly. As soon as he left, my life changed, but that isn't what stopped me drinking, after all it had become a habit right? There is a psychological and physical dependency there.

Who helped me stop? It was me, I stopped me drinking. I didn't want drunkenness and self-pity in my life any more.

The CHANGE is the CATALYST but YOU are the DRIVER.

The change in routine goes hand in hand with Step 2 - HATE IT. I hated drinking because it was taking my life away from me. In the following chapter, I list many reasons why we should hate being dependent on drink, and you can think of more I am sure.

1. You have to change your routine: this is the CATALYST

2. Remove the bad influence or factor in your life

3. Then you can move on to dealing with hating the habit so much you will not even want to hear the word "drink" again.

A bit like when you were a child and your parents would say every night: Have you done your homework?"

The word "homework" almost becomes painful to our ears. Just like in adult life when you say: "I can't, I'm working" or "I have to go to work"! Work, work, work. It becomes one of your least liked words. Because you resent it. It makes you miss out on fun times. It makes you get up early every day. It makes you be in a place when you'd rather be somewhere else. You begin to resent "work".

This is what will happen in Step 2, you will resent "drink" because "drink" will be stopping you from having a life, from having fun or being somewhere else you'd rather be.

For now though you must face your fear. This mountain, whatever your mountain may be, must be identified and climbed. It could be a past failure or painful experience. A loss. Your lack of focus or success in life. Just take it on, be honest and admit the reason or reasons for why you are drinking.

You can only deal with a problem when the problem has a form or a name, otherwise it is extremely hard to manage.

For now you accept that you have come to depend on alcohol. You may not be an alcoholic in the conventional sense, i.e. you have a drink as soon as you wake up – in fact the thought of that may make you wince, but there is no denying that you are "alcohol-dependent."

Everything you do now revolves around alcohol.

You wait for the next moment you can have a drink to take that "edge" of your day, to help you feel more relaxed, to help you find peace and be a happier more sociable version of yourself.

Unfortunately over time alcohol no longer makes you more sociable and more relaxed. It is making you angrier. You are a negative aggressive drinker at parties. Instead of feeling relaxed you are now experiencing bloating or knots in your stomach as the alcohol has ravaged the lining of your stomach.

You are looking older as alcohol has destroyed your body's ability to absorb nutrients.

You are no longer Wonder Woman, Mother made in Heaven, Divine Goddess of Sexiness, you are hung out to dry, snapping, depressed, agitated, poorer, unfit…. that's enough, let's carry on with identifying your trigger instead of beating you down!

Example of why you may be dependent on drink:

Accepting failure as the easier option to trying to succeed

You are more comfortable dropping the dreams and ambitions you had as a younger woman, because you would rather stick with your current lifestyle, even though you hate it, than risk failing again.

It is more appealing to you to ignore your aspirations for success or goals to create something beautiful and simply stick your head in the sand to avoid disappointment.

You want to keep your head there in the sand, you don't want to stick your neck out and draw attention to yourself. You think you are passed it. You no longer have the self–belief you once did. You have had more experience in failure at work than success so you'd rather just slunk away into the shadows, pour a glass of wine and use that as your armour against the world or as your cushion to muffle the sounds of your own disappointment. Drink is your shielding cushion against a world that is full of possibilities and change and opportunities that you do not even want to think about.

You are far more comfortable hiding behind your glass, reliving scenes of your past failures (in marriage, at work, bad decisions, poor choices).

Well of course you are going to fail if all you do is relive and rehash the failures of your life. Many of us relive the moments of our past over and over again. We think: "Oh, if only I had done it like this. I should have done that differently. I shouldn't have married him. I shouldn't have left my job". So many I wish I had nots and I wish I hads.

Think in the past = Live in the past. Your thoughts are the instigators of your actions.

You will never move forwards if your head is in the past.

Step 1 involves changing your routine. You need to propel yourself into the future.

Why do you think so many gurus from Oprah to Brendon Burchard go on about the importance of visualising your "future identity".

The body and our actions are fuelled and governed by our thoughts.

From the simplest actions of breathing and walking. The brain has to instruct the body to move.

In the same way our thoughts will govern the decisions we take and the paths we choose. If we dwell on the past and negative thoughts, our actions will reflect this negativity. If we think happy thoughts, positive thoughts, our actions will reflect this positivity. It's logical. If you put diesel in a petrol car it won't go, if you fill it with petrol you can zoom away. Fill yourself with positivity.

Anxiety stemming from over-worry and negative thoughts about oneself will quickly lead to a suppressed pattern of behaviour. The complete opposite of happiness and confidence.

To change your routine, you need to change your mindset from the acceptance of failure to the desire to succeed.

If you want to succeed, believe you can succeed and you will succeed.

The brain is a malleable tool that responds to the thoughts that govern it.

You cannot add red dye to a white cloth and expect it to come out blue. You have to add blue to create blue cloth. You have to add happy, positive thoughts to create happy positive actions. You have to think about the "you" that you want to be in order for you to be that version of "you". She will not just appear all on her own. You have to will her into existence.

Change your habits and routine to create the reality you want. Changing your routine and habits will change the way you think. It is important that you grasp this concept so that you can fully appreciate the power of RETRAINING YOUR BRAIN (Step 3) and how to prevent a RELAPSE (final chapter).

Here is a simple EXAMPLE of how easy it is to change the way you think:

You've been in the same bedroom for a couple of years or more. You have added an extension to your home and you move into a new bedroom. The wardrobe is by the door in your new bedroom, instead of by the bed. When you are in the kitchen looking outside, perhaps it is raining or snowing, and you think to yourself: "I need to get my coat from my wardrobe" - your brain will immediately picture your wardrobe where it was in the your *old* bedroom, the one you have been in for years as opposed to just days. When you go to your room, your body will instinctively head towards the bed where the wardrobe used to be.

Even though you know full well and so does your brain, that you are no longer in that old bedroom, it has been conditioned for so long to "knowing" that the wardrobe is next to the bed in your *old* bedroom, not by the door in your *new* bedroom.

It is only after having used your *new* bedroom for a few weeks, or maybe just days, that your brain soon forgets the imprint of the previous layout because it has learned that it will not find a coat or wardrobe there by the bed, because it is by the door in the *new* bedroom. After a few days or weeks, your body will instinctively go by the door in your bedroom to find the wardrobe. Just like with drinking, if you have been a drinker for a long time, you may relapse, as with the bedroom metaphor, from time to time when you are caught off guard you may still veer towards the bed thinking the wardrobe is there.

You have to exercise your brain into living the *new* version of you so clearly that it forgets the *old* version of you or even why you want a drink in the first place!

Picture yourself walking as the future you, shopping, laughing, wearing clothes you like, having a healthy glow, going out in the evenings, swimming, dancing, smiling... picture the future you every day until the day you are the future you.

It all starts with thought. Thoughts are the spring and source of how we manifest ourselves. If our brain says to go backwards, we do not walk forwards. We walk backwards. If your brain says to go forwards, you will move forwards.

Take that first step in changing your routine. Get rid of the physical manifestation of your fears or the trigger/"excuse" for your dependency.

You do not need to be as drastic as I was by "kicking" your problem out of the door. You could have a break from your relationship, he may be needing it too. You may decide to go for counselling.

If your job is getting you down, go and retrain in an area you want to work in. Do not worry what others think of you. If it is what you truly enjoy and what you want. It will be easy to make this decision and to go forward.

If you are unhappy in your job but enjoy the sector you are in, try to find a different placement if you are unhappy in your work environment.

If you were hurt in the past, seek professional help. Get counselling for that specific incident, not for your dependency on alcohol. The dependency is a manifestation of the hurt and unresolved problems created by that incident of pain in your past.

When we are ourselves, our true selves, and when we do what we like to do and what we have a passion for, this makes us feel more confident. We have more confidence in ourselves because we are doing what we enjoy and what is true to us. Being true to ourselves and doing what we believe in deepens our confidence. With greater confidence we are able to get rid of bad habits that are keeping us back. With greater confidence we no longer need to hide behind the mistruths and fickleness of our so-called "friend" alcohol. We are proud to be ourselves.

OWN IT

Whatever your "excuse" or "trigger" for drinking, admit it, face it and handle it.

Once this change is taking place or has taken place, you will feel a huge sense of relief.

21

Now it is time to focus on changing the smaller parts of your everyday life to help support this big change. This big change is not daunting. It is what you want and what you need. It is good for you and therefore it is good for those around you. If you are happier, your family and children will be happier.

This change is not a selfish act.

Wanting to improve yourself is not a selfish act. You will have more of your positivity to share. You will be helping others who you love.

There are 2 smaller steps to be taken under this umbrella of change:

1. You must absolutely change **where** you usually drink – don't go there.

The location is associated with the habit.

This is how I beat all my bad habits the first time for good (a couple of weak moments – check out RELAPSE chapter), but change of location is a great breaker of habits. You want to pick up GOOD habits.

2. Managing your **time**:

There is so much time in the day.

Look at it this way – it was real eye-opener for me:

8 hours sleeping – that's plenty

8 hours working/job – more than enough!

8 hours – YOURS!

So let's say of that last 8 hours you spend 4 hours cleaning, cooking, travelling, miscellaneous chores, etc. That still leaves 4 hours. The 4 hours you used to drink away, mong in front of the TV or whatever spaced out activity you chose.

Think of all the stuff you do in 4 hours. Read, write, nap, exercise, draw, make stuff, cook, spa fun, meet friends, walk, go out, play with the children... it is endless.

Here is one example. Not eating to feel the effects of alcohol more. Some of us wait to eat until after I we have had enough drink to make us feel "out of it". This means that dinner time becomes later and later maybe 10 p.m. or midnight became – obviously unhealthy as you may eat and then drop off to sleep. Bad in every way for your diet, figure, digestion, oral hygiene, etc.

What if you were to bring your dinner time forwards? No excuses just do it. You feel less like drinking on a full stomach. Eat at the same time as the children, eat at 6 p.m. or when you get home from work, instead of reaching instantly for the bottle – fewer calories too!

Then you can have your pudding (some fruit and yoghurt or a bowl of cereal) later on at 9 p.m. Or exercise before coming home – hit the gym – it makes you feel positive about yourself.

Change of habits can be easy and effective

And don't dismiss the idea of eating at different times by thinking that you will be eating more to make up for not drinking.... just remember how many calories are in your glass or bottle of wine or gin!!

Besides, you could try to eat a balanced diet, especially before giving up and at the beginning when your body will be craving vitamins (check out Club Soda "The mindful drinking movement" on the Internet for an explanation of exactly what vitamins and minerals you should be taking and even some great tips on how to lessen the effect of cravings).

It may seem peculiar to begin with, but hey, so does eating at midnight!

Later when you have rid yourself of your dependency you can put your eating times to whenever you want.

Each of you will have been riding this rollercoaster of ups and downs for a different length of time. Scurrying through the hectic chaos of everyday life and grabbing for a drink at the end of the day to make it all go away to find that inner peace again.

Below is an example of a hectic routine that gives no leeway for stopping to think about yourself. No time to do what you want to do. It is a perpetual cycle full of triggers to make you want a drink:

Example of a hectic routine:

get up, drink coffee

make pack lunches

get children up and dressed and fed

slap on makeup and get ready

take children to school

go to work

impress everyone at work

go to gym at lunch to fight flab

work long to impress boss

leave late

pick up kids from after school club

get home wash up breakfast stuff

tidy up laundry

yell at kids to do their homework

make dinner

yell at kids to get washed and stop watching so much YouTube

say hi to husband on the sofa

wash up after dinner

say goodnight to kids

pour glass of wine sit on sofa and vegetate

11 pm several glasses later, drag yourself to bed

have a bad night's sleep

wake up and do it all over again

Of course I will have missed stuff out like looking after your parents perhaps, or the weekend chores or doing the garden or making Sunday roast for your in-laws or taking dogs for walk, cleaning out the rabbit's hutch, wiping up the cat's sick, watering the plants, dusting the house, battling the ironing pile, ordering the shopping online, the list goes on forever.

How can you cope? You need to replace the "triggers" of drinking or the "excuses" for drinking. These triggers or excuses include:

> I'm too tired.
> I'll do it tomorrow
> One drink won't hurt me.
> I need this drink.
> I deserve this drink.

If you feel swamped, or undervalued at home or at work, these feelings of low self-worth and defeat will trigger and justify your continued habit of drinking.

I do not pretend to understand your personal circumstances, but I do know that if you have come this far, you know that you are not in control of your life. If you are not in control of it, who is? What are you waiting for? A knight in shining armour? Some miracle that is most likely never going to happen?

Everybody's circumstances are different, it is the core that is the same: loss of faith in yourself, loss of faith in life, lack of direction, lack of purpose, a sense of futility.

In fact, matters could be worse for some of you. Perhaps you started drinking at 5 p.m. or 6 p.m. as soon as you get through the door. It is taking you more and more alcohol to get you to that feeling of fake "rest" you once had. You need more drink to cope. If you are at home all day, you may have even started drinking in the afternoon: "Just one to help me get through." Then you go to pick up the children. You're either driving under the influence or arriving at school hoping no one will smell the alcohol on your breath. Either way, it's not good news. You are no longer in control of yourself. Alcohol is controlling your life.

The more you drink the less of a grip you will have on how to govern your actions and decisions.

You become more weak-willed.

You know that what you are reading is right because you must have been living like this for several months or years now. That is why you have picked up this book.

The bottom line is that you are on an infernal hamster wheel of chores and must-dos. Tension and stress levels are high, you are aging and draining yourself. So here is my suggestion.

What if for those 4 hours in the evening, instead of drinking you were to **do something else**. By taking away the drinking you automatically gain 4 hours in your day. For starters you have a better night's sleep. You will have probably heard countless "experts" say that you'll sleep better without drink, but you don't believe them because alcohol helps you sleep, it makes you feel drowsy and when you didn't drink you had very fitful nights, sweating, tossing and turning. The reason for the latter is because your body is used to drinking and it is coping with not having alcohol in the system.

The reason alcohol as a stimulant does not give you a sound night's sleep is because alcohol metabolizes quickly in our system and disrupts our sleep, thereby impairing the quality of our sleep – not to mention being woken up by our own snoring!![5]

---

[5] "Alcohol reduces sleep latency and results in lighter, disrupted sleep during the second half of the sleep period. Alcohol worsens OSA*." Source: Atlas of Clinical Sleep Medicine, by Meir H. Kryger (*Obstructive Sleep Apnea)

If you sleep better, you will probably wake up earlier, which means you have gained an hour or two in the morning.

Secondly, without the friends of Mr Hangover or Mr Depletion hanging around you the next day, you can get your work done so much more efficiently; you will not have to work late. This will not only impress your boss more, but it will free up time you can spend with your children.

Instead of yelling at them to do their homework whilst you are preparing that lean lasagne, you will be able to do it with them.

Do something else

NEW ROUTINE So here is how your day could look instead:

wake up feeling refreshed at 6 a.m.

1 hour for you time:

     meditate, yoga, walk, or jog or cycle, long shower and get dressed.

wake up children (and partner?) help them get dressed and washed

have breakfast together!

take them to school

go to work (you can still go to the gym at lunch)

pick up children from school instead of a club, (pick up shopping)

or walk to pick them up

let your children unwind

     - talk to you about school, have a snack whilst you prepare dinner.

     - let them play , go out or do homework – help them

     - take the dog out for a walk together

6 p.m. put dinner out together, enjoy it together

do the washing up – make lunch for tomorrow

spend time on YOU –

     your personal projects/spa or personal wellness time/read

spend time with your PARTNER

go to an evening's class or unwind:

     meditate, draw, watch a movie, write to/skype your family,

go to a help group, take a bath, learn a skill...

11 p.m. go to bed tired for the right reasons

6 a.m. wake up refreshed, bursting to see what the day will bring ☺

If you finish your day disappointed with yourself that is how you will start the next day.

Each day you conquer your obstacles, makes the next day just that bit easier to conquer your battles.

It may seem impossible at first, but give it a try. What have you go to lose by trying to change for the better?

The more you fill your mind with wanting to change and ways to change, the more you will act upon these thoughts and information. Just as you did when you filled yourself with despair and negativity, you reacted with actions that reflected your thoughts of "I can't", "I need to drink", "What's the point", etc.

Now replace these thoughts with: "I can, I can, I want to feel great, I want my life back, I want to feel good about myself, I want more energy..."

Your brain can be reprogrammed.

If you are interested, here is an example of **my daily routine**:

Wake up around 5am or 6am

Make lemon and ginger tea, feed and stroke cat, open up the blinds

Stretch/yoga, breakfast, shower, plan my day - I love my mornings!

Make kids lunch, see them off

9 a.m. to 11 a.m. MY WORK I write, draw or whatever I am into at the time

go out for coffee with a friend or go shopping (I cycle or walk) / jog

lunch

Work that I enjoy

Make dinner, tend to the plants, garden, house

Eat with the children

Read in front of fire, plan trips/yoga/friends out in the garden

Paint, write or watch a movie

Skype friends, family, plan projects

Go sleep at 11 p.m. happy, grateful and looking forward to tomorrow

Be excited about your day, don't dread it.

Do not worry, after reading this short guide you will no longer be caught up on the hamster wheel of futility. Just by thinking of stopping you have already made a switch in your brain. Let's move on to real crutches that are not fickle and will genuinely help you take the next steps to a clearer, more energised and focussed life where your dreams are achieved and you feel a sense of happiness and worth every day.

GETTING THROUGH THE FIRST WEEK TOGETHER[6]

DAY 1

Great! You have decided to quit poisoning yourself.

Now empty every single bit of drink down the drain. Take a photo of yourself so you can remind yourself of what not to go back to!

Do not give your alcohol to someone or hide it somewhere – your moments of weakness will make you go back to that person or that place and find the bottle again.

Empty it all away. There must be nothing to tempt you.

Tell your partner/spouse not to drink. If they love you, they will stop with you – this is important at the beginning. If they disagree, go stay with someone for a week who will help you get through this. Or maybe take a look at your relationship!

This is the easy day – the day that you are filled with determination. So no treats and no rewards. Just keep reminding yourself when the craving comes, that it will go away. And it will get easier. If it is bad, try some of my tips, such as a bath with lemon oil, exercise, your favourite movie, spa treatment - anything to distract you.

DAY 2

You will have woken up feeling tired. That is because you are actually sleeping properly.

---

[6] Remember to be honest with yourself: If you are a heavy drinker you will need professional assistance to get through this period of detox as you will suffer from nausea, vomiting, shaking, painful headaches, unsettled sense of anxiety and agitation. Go to your GP, they will be able to refer you or help you with a prescription to help you through the physical side-effects of first week.

Fill yourself early on with lots of vitamin C. Your body's balance will be readjusting. Help it to heal. Drink a lot of water and juice. Your body will feel dehydrated due to the diuretic effect of alcohol.

Today and tomorrow are potentially when your physical symptoms will peak.

Tonight is tougher than Day 1, so make a nice meal, eat earlier, buy some nice clothes with the £10 or £20 you saved.

The first 48 hours are hard so fill your mind with positive influences. Get support and encouragement from your family, watch videos online to reinforce the positivity of what you are doing and the benefits, read books (like this one) on how you will feel so much better.

Fuel the positive impressions in your mind. Fill your body with plenty of water, juice and Vitamin-C rich foods.

DAY 3

You will be feeling more rested after a proper nights' sleep.

Now you can feel the benefits, it should be easier to convince yourself to keep going.

If you are feeling up to it, celebrate your achievement by sharing your news with friends, inviting them around to play a game, watch a film, go out for a meal. Let others support you. Even if you can't or don't want to go to groups like the AA, there are plenty of online forums where you can chat and get help and share experiences with other women in the same position. This process can really bolster your confidence.

The very fact that you are anonymous on these forums can really help you to be more open and therefore deal with the problem honestly, instead of making further excuses for yourself.

Talk to the other women, share the fact that it is hard. Congratulate them. Strength in numbers: you will encourage each other and forge online friendships that will save you from drinking.

You may find that browsing and forums becomes your new *good* habit in the evening!

DAY 4

You're over the "hump". You feel like you have accomplished something, so you may want to indulge in just one teeny-weeny glass of wine or beer.

DON'T!! One glass is never one glass, it always leads to 2 or 3 or more.

Now is a good time to take a break away – a holiday home in the middle of nowhere with long walks and a hot tub.

Being in a new place will take your mind off it.

If you can't, burn some lavender oil or neroli oil to lift your spirits. If your headaches are still persisting book yourself in for an Indian head massage. An amazing experience. You can afford it from what you have saved by not drinking.

Your are just getting into the swing of what psychologists call the **competence confidence**. This means that the better you get at something, the more confident you will feel about it.

The better you get at abstaining from drink, the better you will feel about yourself. Your confidence levels will rise. With greater confidence you have less need for that "excuse" of drink. You can be yourself without hiding. You can deal with work and the house without alcohol.

You make sure you get through Day 4. You are over half way.

DAY 5

You will be feeling one of two things:

1. You want your comfort blanket back because you are fearing this change, you are fearing loosing all that cloud and drunken haze you used to be able to hide behind. You fear making steps towards a new future because it is an unknown future.

If this is the case, focus on enjoying each step that is involved in this change. Soon all the steps will add up to become your new routine, your new set of habits, and drinking will be the thing of the past. Drinking will be the change you left behind.

Enjoy the steps of tasting and savouring your meals, enjoy being able to wake up and function without feeling sick or grumpy, enjoy having at least £25* if not £50 more in your purse or bank account.

*Cheap wine at £5 a bottle, or nicer stuff or spirits, times 5 days.

Or you may be feeling:

2. Wow this is great I feel so much better, it actually is not that hard. I wish I had done this earlier.

Right, what can I tackle next. I am so excited about my day. I can't wait to get going.

Hopefully you will be feeling number 2. But if you are feeling number 1, just take a look at yourself in the mirror:

Your face should no longer be as red as it was, other skin conditions such as eczema and dandruff should have improved too. On the scales you are most likely a few pounds lighter even without trying.

Look back to your photo on day 1 – can you see the improvement?

You will look more hydrated and alive!

Go on a long walk – half an hour at least. Listen to music. Look at the landscape around you. Absorb life. Be a part of this world.

DAY 6

YOUR DAY!

Make it all as stress-free as possible. Clear this day of all commitments – as much as you can.

Today is the day to be mindful – a buzzword thrown around these days. I mean it in its pure form and meaning: look after yourself. Be upfront with everyone if you can, it will make everything easier. Tell everyone you want to stop drinking. Or if you are embarrassed, tell them you are on a week of "mindfulness". This will be helpful to your employer, your family, your partner and most importantly you. So take the day off. Fill it only with stuff you like and want to do. DO NOT do the housework or other chores! It will all be there tomorrow, the world will not collapse – or maybe someone else will have done it for you!

Do some exercise, a Zumba class or for a run, start that gym or Pilates class, your body will be in much better shape than at the beginning of the week. There shouldn't be a risk of hot flushes and sudden sweating anymore! Physical exercise helps to oxygenate your body. You will feel alive!

DAY 7

You won't be able to see all the wonderful healing processes going on inside your body but your liver is now thanking you. It can filter out the toxins from your body and is not overloaded with fat (hence the healthier glow to your skin). Your risk of oral and other cancers is now on the decline instead of on the rise.

Other than the physical improvements and great clarity and focus, there is something you will definitely be able to see: the bigger number in your bank account.

Example: £5 per night every night = £1,825 saved in a year

Plus, if you went out twice a week and spent £20 each time (£2,080) then you will have **saved almost £4,000!!!** (£3,905 to be exact)

Keep up with the walking and/or exercise sessions – at least 3 times a week. This will help to detox your body and it will increase your motivation and drive to stay alcohol-free.

1 week – Great job! Repeat the days that worked well for you

By repeating something you get better at it. As mentioned before: competence confidence.

DRINKING STEALS YOUR LIFE

RECLAIM YOUR LIFE

You used to be a pro at drinking, but after you changed your routine you're a pro at being confident and going after your dreams.

Repetition and practise are key. Sound familiar?

Just as with anything that you practise you get better at it. For example, learning to play the piano – even if you practice just 5 minutes every day, you'll be able to read the notes by the end of a week.

Want to learn a new language? Every time you learn a new word you are closer to learning how to string a sentence together. After one sentence comes another and then anther, soon you'll be able to speak that language.

Remember how you didn't know how to cook or how to ride a bike or how to drive? Now you probably drive and can ride a bike because you practiced.

Practise your *good* habits every day and they will become natural to you.

Increase your competency in forming good habits and they will become second nature to you – just like learning to read, learning to swim or memorising your favourite song.

Repetition is key.

You've managed 1 week, now do week 2.

Force yourself at the beginning if your pesky fickle ego is telling you not to. Do not stop to think (sorry Mel Robson, I disagree with your theory of pausing before doing something, you risk talking yourself out of it) just go on automatic pilot and do it.

Do your morning routine without stopping to think: "I don't want to" or "It's too cold outside" or "I'll just have another 5 minutes in bed".

Just do it. Yes, the Nike slogan. Why do you think the company is so successful!! Just do it!

If you stop to think, you'll definitely talk yourself out of it. Your brain has not been retrained so it will find the easy way out.

Don't listen to it. Train it to be a better version of itself.

Not a drinker but an achiever and self-believer.

A little note – don't go crazy with stuff to do

You do not have to cram your day full of "other stuff" to do. A helter-skelter approach will fizzle out a month or two or a year or two down the line and you are more likely to relapse.

Only fill your day/time with stuff you actually want to do.

Spending more time getting in touch with yourself will make the long-term success more achievable and concrete.

Having solid roots is essential. If you just have great flowers and leaves for a year but don't look after your roots, when summer comes next year, you won't blossom again, you'll wither.

Whilst diverting your thoughts and actions away from the act of drinking may be beneficial to you at the beginning so that you literally do not have time to drink, you must beware of simply filling your life with distractions.

Keep a focus on why you were drinking in the first place. That issue, trigger or "excuse" as I call it, has to be dealt with and resolved. Do not run away from yourself. Going from one activity to the next without thought will ultimately lead to you burning yourself out and starting right back at the beginning, whether it is after a few months or even years. Deal with your issues as outlined in part one of this book. Face your excuses and reasons for drinking.

Make sure that what you are doing is in line with what you are thinking. When your thoughts and actions are working in harmony, you are at peace with yourself. You find strength in this unity. This strength will give you confidence. With confidence you become an invincible force.

Do not hide behind more excuses that mask your fears. Do not simply act out the wishes of others. Your routine and your changes have to be yours.

Follow the routine on page 28 or even better write out your own. In week 2, remember to reward yourself on Day 3 and Day 6 – use the money saved, keep a check on your physical improvements, congratulate yourself and enjoy the sense of empowerment. Plus you may have made some new friends or joined a class. Or maybe learned a new skill. Whatever path you chose make sure it is one you enjoy – and remember to do what makes you happy.

OWN IT

RECLAIM YOUR LIFE

You can find calm and unity through thoughtfulness, meditation, mindfulness - the principles of yoga.

Some of these suggestions may seem too "hippy" or "alternative" for you. You do not have become a Buddhist or hum for 15 minutes every morning in the lotus position. You can manage the art of unity in your own way.

Perhaps art, dance or music gives you this sense of focus and calm. Jogging or swimming may be where you find your peace. You need to look inside yourself to find this calm and focus. Find your way there. As with all things in life, it is about the journey not the end destination. You will be strong if you do things that reflect your inner nature.

Like a table with four legs. It only works if all four legs are stable. Take away one leg and the table collapses. It no longer serves as a table. It is just pieces of wood. In the same way, you need to bring cohesion to yourself. Make sure that what you are thinking and doing marry up and are in alignment.

You will be off-balance if you are acting contrary to how you are feeling. If your actions contradict your beliefs and convictions, you will fall off the path you want to be on. To stay on that path of giving up drinking and becoming the version of "you" you want to become, you must be at peace with your inner self.

Suggestion: Refer back to the suggested daily routine above. Start every morning with thought. Feed your brain through exercise (a brisk walk, stretching, jogging) and write down what you want to be. Write down what you want to achieve. This works better for some people instead of meditation.

Your actions will follow your thoughts. Do not let your actions be fruitless and without direction.

If you fill your day with actions to divert your attention from drinking, make sure these actions are part of the plan to keep you who you want to be.

I noticed when learning to play the piano, if I tried to learn a piece all in one go, i.e. both left and right hand together, I would end up stumbling over the same areas that were tricky for me. Whereas if I broke the piece down into sections and learnt each piece separately so well that it became second nature to my fingers (muscle memory through repetition), then when it came to playing the entire piece together, it flowed smoothly. The piece virtually played itself.

If you learn to master each piece of your problem, tackle each part individually and master it, then when it comes to putting your life together, it works harmoniously together – like the piano piece, like the four legs of the table. Working in unity.

Step 2

HATE IT

Loathe the bad habit

Demonise drinking

You have to hate drinking so much that your hate overrides your cravings.

This concept ties in with Step 3: BEAT IT. To beat your addiction you will be retraining your brain. The initial part of this retraining is to associate negativity with drinking instead of that false promise of relaxation, escape and happiness.

This chapter lists many cons to drinking, many reasons for hating drinking. At the end of this chapter I want you to add any more of your own personal reasons for hating drinking, i.e. what you have not been able to do or achieve because of your drinking habit, or maybe what drinking makes you do that you would not do if you were sober.

These will be your vital crutches when your cravings come. Any time you are tempted to drink, your mind will call upon these crutches and let the craving pass. How?

With this simple phrase:

"I really want a drink, but I really don't want...: (here comes your list of reasons why you hate drinking)."

Your hate for what a drink represents will override your craving for a drink. Suddenly your stomach will churn at the thought of a drink.

I hated drinking so much I was disgusted by it.

Once I had ended my sour relationship, I never wanted to touch a drop again.

To me all that badness was interconnected.

Drink represented failure and pain.

After a few years of not drinking, I decided to have a glass of wine with friends since I didn't feel I had to abstain completely and because I felt so much more in control of my life and the direction I was going in.

Well what a surprise.

That first drink which I thought was going to melt through my body, make me giggle and brighten my cheeks did... absolutely nothing.

Nothing. It had no effect, I didn't enjoy it. It didn't taste nice or how I remembered it. A juice would have tasted better or even a fizzy pop drink. I was a shocked as you are.

It was as if my mind controlled the effect the drink was having on my body; it did nothing – by the way, the same happened with my smoking habit. One day I thought I'd try one again to get that "hit". Nothing. Absolutely nothing.

I no longer needed these "vices". They no longer had any effect on me whatsoever.

You too can put your habit to rest by demonising the drink.

DEMONISING DRINK

be disgusted by the habit – hate it

it is stopping you from achieving

it is taking up all your money

it is taking money from your family

you can't remember what happened

you look like shit

you get blinding headaches

you're not getting promoted at work

As soon as you think: "I don't want to be drinking" throw your drink away. You may hate yourself and think: "What a waste", but I guarantee you that in the morning and every day thereafter, you will be grateful for your actions. The long-term benefits outweigh the short-term yearnings.

What does drinking actually do for you?

Look at the reverse side if you are sceptical.

Think of the pros of drinking before we move on to the cons.

In my mind there are not many pros:

<u>Drink relaxes you for a couple of hours.</u>

And then what?

I am really struggling to think of any pros to drinking that are not automatically associated with a negative in my mind.

At what expense are you "relaxing for a couple of hours"? The next 16 hours of your day will be completely lost. You will not be able to drive, sleep well, communicate effectively, remember having a good time, be productive, exercise, and so on.

This might be another pro:

<u>Drink removes my inhibitions</u>

You feel that you like to drink because suddenly you have more courage to be yourself. You are more relaxed, less tense, the filter on your mouth is removed, you say what you feel instead of holding it in and bottling it up. But this release for inhibitions is a false sense of courage.

What if I were to tell you that you could be yourself, feel confident and say what you believe without the help of drink? And it would be all day every day not just when you drink?

If you follow your path (as outline in the previous chapter), if your actions reflect your thoughts, if you are true to yourself then you will naturally feel more confident about yourself. Nobody can blow over a tree with strong roots. Build your foundations through being yourself and being true to yourself through your choices and actions in life.

It is because you are not happy with your situation that you turn to drink. You think it is easier just to stay in this unhappy situation because pulling yourself out of it seems harder.

You are wrong.

By drinking and avoiding your unhappiness, you are feeling more hurt and more negativity than you can bear. The pain you feel now is greater than the small amount of effort it will take to change your life into a happy situation.

It is all about choice.

You need to take small steps to make big changes. The bricks used to build a tower, sky scraper or the pyramids are proportionally tiny compared to the overall edifice they create.

Your tiny steps can create your tower of strength. Tiny steps, tiny bricks can create big results.

Can you think of any more pros to drinking? Any pros that are not naturally affiliated with a con?

I can't.

The hurt you feel hiding away from the opportunities life is full of is a much greater strain on you (both body and soul) than the effort it takes to change your life. Those tiny steps that will create a beautiful happy life, one where you do not need drink to relax at the expense of damaging your liver, kidneys and brain cells. You can find relaxation through satisfaction in your actions, through accomplishment, through something as simply as a spa session, 20 minutes walking in the woods, taking a mini-holiday, creating something.

Drink is stopping you from relaxing. It is stopping you from living. It is stopping you from having the courage to be yourself.

Drink is the fickle friend that provides only empty promises and delivers pain.

Pain in the form of physical damage to your body and depressing effects on your mind (Drink Aware provides a very clear and succinct explanation as to how alcohol is a depressant in chemical terms and is in fact a fickle friend promising relief from anxiety when instead it is increasing your anxiety[7]).

If you want drugs, make your own happy drugs naturally. The following list of natural ways to release "happy hormones" into your system is based on research from "Mind Body Green[8] - next page.

---

[7] "Our brains rely on a delicate balance of chemicals and processes. Alcohol is a depressant, which means it can disrupt that balance, affecting our thoughts, feelings and actions – and sometimes our long-term mental health. This is partly down to 'neurotransmitters', chemicals that help to transmit signals from one nerve (or neuron) in the brain to another.

The relaxed feeling you can get when you have that first drink is due to the chemical changes alcohol has caused in your brain. For many of us, a drink can help us feel more confident and less anxious. That's because it's starting to depress the part of the brain we associate with inhibition.

But, as you drink more, more of the brain starts to be affected. It doesn't matter what mood you're in to start with, when high levels of alcohol are involved, instead of pleasurable effects increasing, it's possible that a negative emotional response will take over. Alcohol can be linked to aggression you could become angry, aggressive, anxious or depressed."
Source: Drink Aware

[8] Source: www.mindbodygreen.com

1. Endorphins

Endorphins are opioid neuropeptides produced by the central nervous system to help us deal with physical pain. One way to induce endorphins is through exercise.

Endorphins are released after both aerobic and anaerobic exercise. In one study, as little as 30 minutes of walking on a treadmill for 10 days in a row was sufficient to produce a significant reduction in depression among clinically depressed subjects.

2. Serotonin

Serotonin may be the best-known happiness chemical. It is a neurotransmitter that is naturally triggered through exposure to bright light, especially sunshine, exercise and happy thoughts and also a higher intake of tryptophan-heavy foods.

3. Dopamine

Dopamine is a neurotransmitter often referred to as the "chemical of reward", i.e. when you get good grades, score a goal, get great feedback, etc., you can also get a natural dose of dopamine when you perform acts of kindness toward others.

4. Oxytocin

Mothers are familiar with oxytocin, the hormone produced in abundance during pregnancy and breastfeeding, primarily associated with loving touch and close relationships.

This list shows just how easy it can be to find more of a happy balance in your life. Remember, drink is a dead-end fix. It is not the solution. It is the problem.

Now let's try once again to think of those pros.... Nope, only more reasons for hating drink spring to mind:

It ages your body

you cannot heal, regenerate

your complexion is dulled

it makes other bad habits easier (e.g. smoking, gambling)

it makes you put on weight (calories)

you cannot absorb nutrients

it stops you exercising

your hands are swollen

your hands shake

your face/nose is constantly red

you are bloated

Keratosis in your mouth (bad gums/poor oral hygiene)

dulled mind – cannot react or learn

kidney failure

you are a burden to your family

you become self-absorbed

you do not notice what is going on around you

your children are growing up without you

you are a bad role model for your children

you don't have much money, no savings.

You don't have to give up for your sake – you can give up for the sake of others. People you may currently love more than yourself. Sometimes it is easier to make big changes for the sake of others, than it is just for yourself.

See what a difference it will make when you have more time to spend with your children. When you can talk to them in the morning instead of barking at them because you have a hangover or are grumpy and irritable. See how chatting positively in the morning brightens up the whole day. Their behaviour will change because you can cope, because you are showing them love. This will alleviate the stress you feel in your home life.

You shall reap what you sow.

If you give off bad vibes and grumpiness what do you expect your children to give you in return? They are (just as we all are) a reflection of their environment. Give them love and a smile and they will have no choice but to be loving back - you may need to give a bit more allowance during their teenage years! Those hormones can be unpredictable but you can cope with it so much better with a clear head and a happy mind.

Just imagine the joy you would feel of going to bed or waking up knowing that instead of drinking that night you had made a step (a tiny brick was laid) towards realising your dreams and aspirations. You had made a step *towards* instead of *away* from living the life of your dreams.

Now compare that feel-good feeling with waking up or going to bed feeling nauseous, a bad headache, thirsty, tired, de-energised.

You really don't have to think too hard to hate your dependency on drink.

When and if you do have a drink (see also the final chapter on Relapse) you will find that you are forcing yourself back into your bad habit. Because you have seen just how much you can achieve without it and how good you feel without it, it will not have the same effect on you. You will try to drink to get that "relaxed" feeling but it simply won't come. What manifests instead is the awareness that without the drink, you can accomplish so much more. Because you have learned to hate drink and seen it for the fickle friend it is; you will fear drinking. Drinking will become your enemy.

It will be demonised as the act that stops you from living and only gives you a diminished version of yourself that cannot act, think or respond as brilliantly and quickly as the you without drink.

Write down your reasons for **hating drink**. Use those listed in this guide (page 49) if they apply to you, and feel free to add some of your own.

makes me forget costs a lot

puts on weight bad role model

makes me tired depletes energy

makes me sad loses confidence

heavy burden bad for driving

stops me being embarrasing

+ having fun killing me!

Each word on the page gets you one step closer to DEMONISING your habit.

One step closer to BEATING your habit.

Step 3

BEAT IT

Repetition and reward

Retrain the brain

Luckily alcohol comes with its own HATE ME features.

The previous chapter clearly shows this.

It is an easy habit to hate.

Unlike smoking where you cannot actually feel the cancer growing inside you when you inhale, when you drink you can feel the effects just a few hours later; for example, when you wake up in the middle of the night dying for a pee, have a pounding headache, palpitations and a mouth like a camel's arse. You don't have to wait long for the nasty negative effects to rear their ugly heads!

Let your body get used to be being without alcohol.

Continue the demonization process as you move into the BEATING IT phase. Realise that every time you drink you are

- disappointing yourself

- moving further away from fulfilling your dreams and aspirations

- making yourself comatose

- are in for a bad night's sleep

- aging your body

- missing out on physical exercise which will make you happier

- spending money you'll piss down the toilet

- could be saving money

- could be improving your health

- missing out on a better quality of life

- setting a bad example for your children

- becoming unfocussed

- being incoherent

- going backwards

- lying to yourself

- taking the coward's way out

- you are missing out

What are you missing out on by being drunk? Well if you were more aware you might know. You may be inebriated when your children are crying out for help but you don't notice the signs, for days, for weeks... You may be missing out on thoughts and opportunities, you may have otherwise have had if your head wasn't so mashed. Perhaps you are forgetting things without realising it – like updates, filing forms, school appointments, open days, meetings, etc.

Start the momentum, set up the ladder and climb your mountain

You have to take that first step to get to the next step, to get to the next step on your climb up to the top. You need momentum to keep propelling you up and up, on and on.

Each day without drink has to be seen as an achievement, especially during the first 7 days of detox. You need to reward yourself.

Part of your Reward Programme can be simply monitoring the benefits of giving up:

- Weigh yourself at the beginning and each day see how much weight you have lost or didn't put on.

- Take a photo of yourself the day you stop and another after a week to see how your skin has improved.

- Set up a savings account the day you stop and set up an automatic transfer for every day at the amount you would have spent on alcohol, watch it tot up! Do not enter the amount yourself every day otherwise this will remind you of drink – just check the balance in your savings when you want encouragement or cheering up.

- Make an inspiration board. Print out photos of great holidays, places you want to go see, you when you were looking "hot", your children (preferably smiling) and anything else that inspires you or makes you smile (art, cute animals, plants, architecture, cars, anything). You can store this on your phone or computer if you prefer to keep it private. Or even make a physical dream board to hang on your wall.

- Keep a diary of the changes you have noticed, just bullet points, like, "Dinner was delicious, so much better than a salty take-out", "Didn't feel tired today", "Didn't feel tearful", "I felt more confident", "Totally crushed it at the gym", "Felt pleased with myself", "Watched a movie and remembered the ending", "Started reading again, loving it!". Your Detox Journal is proof of your progress. You can even make entries of hard days, ways to cope, your thoughts and photos. You can look back and see how you felt on good days to help you move forwards.

These "rewards" will help you keep up the momentum.

You must also feel proud of yourself when you have "survived" a craving. When you can look back and think: "Normally I would have had a drink then." You need to say *well done* to yourself. Be proud. It is a good feeling. Remember to stack up those pros and positivity against the cons and negativity.

Drink is not your crutch, it is your ball and chain.

You may have felt liberated, or more confident when you drank but then you needed more and more to get that feeling. After a while that feeling of lightheaded bliss was no longer achievable and you just kept drinking out of habit hoping it would all go away and something or someone will miraculously come and save you. Well, I've got news for you: you're the one that has come to miraculously save yourself!

Why can't it be you that achieves the impossible? Why can't you play the superhero or knight in shining armour? It's your life. Be the star in it.

BEAT IT

REWARD YOURSELF

Although the benefits you will get from stopping are rewarding in themselves, your brain will demand more. It will say: "This has been bloody hard work. What do I get in return?" Reward your brain with stuff you crave other than alcohol or other drugs – so something nice to wear, a trip out or evening out, a makeover, a massage.

You must reward yourself otherwise your will power may just go on strike!

Just because you fail giving up the first or may be even the third time, doesn't mean you give up. Keep going. Your mind and your thoughts are geared and ready to stop. Chip away at your weakness. Chip away at the bad side of you that influences the good you want to achieve. You will eventually wear her down and break the habit.

Keep going.

Soon you'll be free from the shackles of alcohol and be able to breathe the fresh air, sleep the good sleep, feel rested, energised and focussed.

Doesn't that in itself make it worth it? Aside from all the chasing dreams, saving money and wasted time? Wouldn't you just like to feel good again?

Fill your head with POSITIVE influences. There are some great motivators to look up online if you are not part of a self-help group:

- doing something new

- going somewhere new

- being a role model

- having an objective to work towards

- compliment yourself

- being outdoors

- communicating openly

- music, art, exercising

You are what you think. Your thoughts become actions.

JUST A THOUGHT

What did you do before you drank?

You are still the same person. You may have played different roles through life, like the role of daughter, sister, girlfriend, wife, boss, teacher, work colleague, acquaintance, friend and so on, but you are the same person inside. You are the constant element throughout all these years. And that version of you did not always drink.

Even if your name has changed, your hair is a different colour, the shape of your body is different; these are all external factors. These external influences do not penetrate into the constant essence of you. All those attributes that make you an individual, that make you different from others. These attributes are yours and yours alone. You must find your way back to them.

Find your way to the constant elements throughout all the years of change and external influences.

Once you find "you", you will find calm. With calm comes peace. With peace comes understanding.

The need to rush around and act impulsively will drop away. You will no longer be fire-fighting. When you find your inner calm you will see life more clearly and be able to judge your dependency for what it really is:

A bad habit you do not need or want.

A bad habit that is ruining your life.

A bad habit that has taken over the essence of you.

A bad habit that has buried the true you under layers of negativity and pain.

It may sound corny but you need to find your inner self. Your constant true self, the girl that has been with you through thick and thin, the girl that can shine, the girl that wants to be happy.

Let this girl be happy. Stop hiding behind the excuse of drink. Give yourself a chance to be happy.

Through thought you can drive away this dependency on alcohol.

The brain is a powerful tool. Use it.

Just as your brain is telling you that drinking will solve all your problems – or at least make them go away for a while – so it will be able to tell you that drinking is bad for you that it is time to stop.

How does this work?

One simple concept: Train the brain

TRAIN THE BRAIN

Just like your brain was "trained' into believing that drinking was a good idea, you can train it to believe the reverse. You started this process in the DEMONISING stage.

Why did my brain think that drinking was a good idea? You may ask. Because when you had a drink in the past it felt good. This "happy" and "relaxed" feeling was released into your neurological system and your nervous system sent messages to your brain telling it that your body was relaxed and your mind was eased. Your brain was being told that the drink was smoothing out all the creases of your day and replacing them with a stress-free happy sensation. Your brain did not associate the blinding headaches and stomach pains as part of this "relaxation" process. Those feelings came afterwards – mostly the next day.

The drink, let's say for argument's sake a glass of wine, triggers this sensation of unwinding then the brain will naturally instruct you to have a glass of wine the next time you are feeling tired and stressed.

Stress -> wine -> happy

It is as simple as that. The brain is trying to protect you and keep you happy.

You need to retrain your brain:

Wine -> feeling sick -> stressed, tired

Handle stress -> relax, happy -> feel great

When you remove alcohol dependency from your life, you will automatically alleviate much of the stress in your life. The alcohol is part of this endless cycle of trying to cope, not being able to cope, drinking, feeling tired, experiencing hangovers and low energy levels.

When you remove alcohol from this cycle your energy levels will rise, which will give you so much more power and focus to deal with the tasks ahead of you at work and at home.

And because you have sought this guide for help, it shows that drinking itself is a "stress factor" in your life. Your habit of drinking is adding stress and worry to your thoughts and stress is one of the main reasons you are turning to drink. Which is why you want to stop.

Does this not seem like an easy paradox to break?

Stop drinking, stop stressing.

You need to prove to your brain that drinking does not fix the problems you are having. Drinking **IS** the problem you are having.

Go back to the first step of changing your routine. You need to create good habits that become your new routine. Your brain will then revert your actions to these "good habits". Retraining your brain to show the positive effects of these good habits (exercise, yoga, meditation, a sense of accomplishment after spending quality time with your family or making progress in your personal projects, etc.) and the rest is easy. Your brain will say NO to the reaching out for a drink. It will remember that the "good habits" lead to your happiness. It will protect you with your "good habits" and not the false friend of drink.

There is scientific research and evidence to back this pattern of behaviour:

"The brain's amygdala is associated with memory and emotion. Certain "cues" are stored as positive or negative memories. For example, let's suppose someone always comes home and fixes a drink. Coming home, and the time (finishing work) now serve as cues to drink because these cues are stored as a positive memory associated with alcohol. When someone tries to stop drinking, these cues serve as powerful motivators to drink despite someone's best intentions to refrain from use. Likewise, people often describe alcohol addiction as a habit, and one that is difficult to break. When people attempt to discontinue an addiction like alcoholism, they can experience withdrawal. The memory of withdrawal is such an unpleasant experience that it serves as a powerful motivator (or cue) to resume the addictive behavior to avoid the unpleasant experience. Eventually, the relief from withdrawal (by resuming use) becomes pleasurable in and of itself. These relapse triggers are due to the amygdala's effect on memory and emotions." (AMHC)

These "cues" are the excuses and triggers you need to take action on, both in giving up and refraining from relapsing.

I believe in "Egolosophy©", studying yourself, finding out what makes you tick, the different inner voices you have goading you on in both positive and negative actions. When you understand yourself, you will understand how to behave and find happiness.

Do not listen to the ego that is tricking you. You do not need the gimmicks of drinking or a sedated, dulled mind to be happy. You have what it takes to be happy and stress free. Alcohol is clouding your judgement. Muddying your clear thoughts.

Don't let your brain and ego be tricked or trick you into a false state of being. The best state of being is BEING YOURSELF. Do not shy away from that. You think it is going to be hard. Your ego tells you that you will fail. You will not. Your ego that tells you to drink is the one making you fail. Stop listening to that voice and free yourself to be yourself. Drop the ball and chain around your happiness and potential calmness.

As you retrain your brain and quieten down that pesky tricky ego of yours, bring up images in your mind of the life you want. Think about your perfect day. Relax into this feeling. What is stopping you from having that perfect day? If you strung a few perfect days together this would soon be a perfect week, which then becomes a perfect month, soon, would you not be on your way to achieving the life you want?

Why are you letting drink drag you down? Why are you letting drink hold you back from happiness?

Don't allow your brain to seek the route of failure just because it seems easier.

Isn't it hard feeling depressed about yourself all the time? Do you not get upset at the fact you cannot control your drinking habit?

Then stop and look to yourself.

Find your inner self. Peel away the layers of influence that the years have had on you and find the happy shiny you inside. Redirect your thoughts to wanting this happiness. Redirect your brain to say "no" to the next drink.

You don't need it.

You tricky ego needs that drink. Let her drink herself into oblivion, heart failure and depression. While you step out of your ego and soar like a phoenix. You are going to be yourself. You are going to be happy.

IT CAN BE SO EASY

You may not believe me, but taking time out, ignoring your brain's directive to drink as your saviour is easier than living in the misery you are in at the moment and have been enduring for so many months, so many years.

On the other side of drink is a happier, younger and brighter you. You do not have to force it. Just make up your mind not to drink. Remind yourself of the things you want in life. It will come to pass. You do not have to force it. Just let go, think good thoughts and say no to drink. Other good things will automatically start appearing in your life. Now you have made space for good things to happen.

Don't let new opportunities pass you by. Open yourself up to life. Open up to calm and close the door to drink. It may not make sense just by reading these words. You have to try it. You have to have faith in yourself. You must believe in yourself. It is in our nature to want to be happy. Your brain will be retrained very easily. Just as easily as it was to start depending on drink. Your brain will seek out the happiness you find without drink. It will want this more because it is more gratifying.

Those 4 extra hours you just found in your day will no longer be wasted on the sofa (literally) or peed down the drain (literally); you will become productive. If not in a physical sense through art or learning, etc., then through the calmness and joy in yourself, knowing that you are in control of your life again. You have more strength, greater clarity and faith in yourself. Remember you are opening up a space that was shut before. Now more positive influences and moments can enter your life.

BEING REALISTIC

Being realistic is not too hard. You cannot expect your life to change in the space of 24 hours... or can you?

If you abstain from drinking and shut that pesky fiend alcohol and that fickle ego of yours out, you will actually feel the benefits straight away.

That is the beauty of the human body.

And from there it only gets better and it only gets easier.

Depending on how much you drink as a regular habit, you may experience physical withdrawal symptoms that are not pleasant:

Even though your body is healing, it is ejecting the toxins and poison so some of the side-effects may include[9]:

- Elevated temperature

- Increased blood pressure, breathing rate, and pulse

- Excessive sweating

- Tremors

- Insomnia

- Irritability

- Poor concentration

These symptoms may appear the next day or after a few days – we are all different and it depends on your genetics, how long and how much you have been drinking, etc. Sometimes you can ride out the storm of detoxing on your own (follow my 7-day plan GETTING THROUGH THE FIRST WEEK TOGETHER, page 31) or you may need professional help. Your GP is a good place to start. They will judge whether you do need to seek medical advice to manage your withdrawal or take prescribed medication to help achieve abstinence or even attend self-help groups, receive extended counselling, or use a talking therapy such as cognitive behavioural therapy (CBT).[10]

Personally, when I gave up, I was not able to concentrate for periods of more than 10 to 15 minutes at the beginning. This was compounded

---

[9] Source: www.quitalcohol.com

[10] www.nhs.uk

because I had also given up other stimulants to my brain (nicotine and caffeine) so my nervous system was detoxifying. It was used to having these chemicals and suddenly I deprived it of all of them (Yippeee!!).

I found that replacing them with naturally generated serotonin from jogging helped speed up the process. Plus increasing my intake of fruit and sleeping longer.

In the end, being realistic is not hard. The sooner your body gets rid of these toxins and poisons, the sooner it will heal and become more energised and your mind will become more focussed.

You may not notice the changes as you go through the transition but if you make a note to stop and take stock of your physical and mental changes after a few days, after a few weeks and after a few months you will see there is actually a **transformation**, not just a transition. Especially if you keep a detox journal.

Bright eyes, clear thoughts, longer periods of focus, quicker reaction times, faster reflexes[11], not to mention more money in the bank account, fresher breath, more energy, less lethargy, fewer headaches (may be some bad ones at the beginning — it is all down to the your individual physiology), better moods, less depressed, easier breathing,

---

[11] According to the National Institutes of Health (NIH), there's strong evidence to suggest that regular binge drinking can damage the frontal cortex and areas of the brain involved in executive functions and decision making. Alcohol slows down the pace of the neurotransmitters in your brain that are critical for proper body responses and even moods.

"Abstaining from alcohol over several months to a year may allow structural brain changes to partially correct," the NIH says. "Abstinence also can help reverse negative effects on thinking skills, including problem solving, memory, and attention." Source: Time Health

more motivation, greater sense of gratitude, and so on and so on.

Picture yourself as a non-drinker.

If you live as a non-drinker in your head you will make staying a non-drinker so much easier. Imagine yourself several *years* down the line. Put yourself in a position of happiness and independence and freedom. Envisage yourself free from drink. If you think that all this effort is just about giving up drinking you are likely to relapse. That may sound confusing, but it is a bit like someone trying to loose weight. How often do they do a fantastic job of losing weight to only put it all back on again later?

You see that a lot right?

That is because the person sees themselves as a fat person. They identify with themselves as someone who is overweight. That is how they have been and how they always will be.

The same applies to you. In order to avoid a relapse you must see yourself as a non-drinker. Do not stop at just giving up drinking. Give up the identity that goes with it.

You have to pave your future with a version of you that you want to be. The version of you that does not drink, who is optimistic, upbeat, energised, ready and willing to achieve success in your relationship, at work and in your personal goals.

If you cannot change your surroundings as I touched upon in Step 1, then you have to change your routine. That is easy to understand, but you must not underestimate how important this is with regards to preventing you from relapsing. When you retrain your brain and envisagea drink-free version of you into the future and beyond, there must be concrete differences in what you do. Changing your actions will change the way you think.

Just as much as the reverse is true, you need to condition your mind through action.

USE THE POWER OF YOUR BRAIN

It's almost effortless.

Have you noticed how you are drawn to certain celebrities? You may be inspired by them, look up to them, want to be like them? Why is that?

The simple answer is because of what they represent to you. They play roles on TV or in films that have inspired you or moved you in some way. Your visual image of them is now associated with a positive feeling in your brain. The halo effect. They look good, they played an incredible character in their last film, they appear strong, always look great, on top of their game - you can finish off this list yourself.

Now your this list and design the "future you" in the same way. Make yourself appealing, someone you want to be. Visualise it. Live it in your mind. Start converting your appearance, your dress sense, new clothes, new haircut, be that person in your mind in real life.

Once you have done this for weeks not just days, you will have created a solid foundation for not relapsing. Plus you will have transformed yourself into a version of you that you like, so why on earth would you want to go back and be that alcoholic-dependent you that is miserable and doesn't enjoy life like you do!?

Side note:

I mention wine a lot because statistics show that most middle-aged women turn to red wine as their main form of drink. "The most popular type of drink for women is wine; according to Office for National Statistics [ONS] figures[...]"[12]

Figure 3: Proportion of average weekly units accounted for by each type of drink among women, 2009, Great Britain

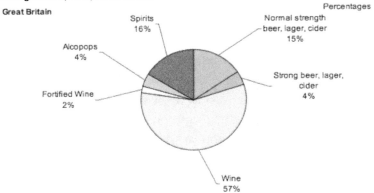

Source: ONS (May 2012), Drinking: Adults' behaviour and knowledge in 2009, 'Statistics on Alcohol: England, 2012'

---

[12] Institute of Alcohol Studies: Women and alcohol Factsheet - Updated May 2013

IN CASE OF A RELAPSE

If you have not properly identified your cues, "triggers" and "excuses" so that you can fight them or if you have not 100% envisaged yourself as a non-drinker, you are most likely going to fail to stay off the drink. The habit will come back if the version of the **future you** has not been fully incorporated in your thoughts and desires and actions. If you have not put those steps in place to make sure your actions will be different then instead of stepping up and away from your habit, you will be walking straight back into it after giving up.

Sometimes the easiest part is actually giving up.

Because you are ready and you are in the right frame of mind and for all the reasons we have covered in the preceding chapters:

You want rid of this habit

This habit disgusts you

You have a drive

You are motivated

You look forward to the rewards

It is something new, a change

and so on

But what happens a year or two down the line when perhaps you are feeling a little low, less motivated, something bad has happened in your life?

You may be going through a personal crisis or a crisis at work or a crisis with your children.

What is going to stop your brain from thinking and convincing you to have a drink?

After all by now a year or two later you'll be feeling all the benefits of having given up:

no more lethargy

more energy

more focus

more motivation

more money

etc.

And so your evil little mind will be saying:

"Go on, remember how relaxing it was. Remember how you used to unwind after just one glass. You need it. You deserve it. Go on have just one or two glasses. It's a one-off I promise."

But we all know the truth. 1 glass is the slippery step to another glass, paving the way for another glass, and another and another and another.

Alcohol reduces your will power. It unlocks the bolts on your self-control and lets it run free. With your self-control running wild you need to reign it back in.

How many times do you think you can do this?

Do you honestly think you can just have one or two glasses and not start the whole pattern of drinking every night all over again?

This is a question you have to answer for yourself. I cannot answer it for you, but I would hazard a guess that in your new time of crisis you will not be able to say NO to starting the habit of drinking again. Your energy levels and will power are already being drained by whatever crisis or emotional upheaval you are experiencing that is driving you back to drink in the first place.

The odds of you being able to find even more energy to give up again are really stacked against you.

My suggestion to you is simply this:

Don't make your life any harder than it already is. As tempting as it may be to relapse and have a few drinks to help smooth out the wrinkles of your life, do not kid yourself. The drink will add to your worries:

1 - You will be more depressed because you are drinking again.

2 - Every night of drinking will bring back the headaches and stomach aches.

3 - You will lose your focus

4 - You will feel demoralised

5 - Your sense of achievement for will go out the window.

You will be the maker of your own demise

Drink will not help you overcome any crisis that you are facing. It will only help you to ignore it. It will only be creating another problem for you to worry over.

You need to look within yourself. When the moment of temptation appears and those words: "Oh to hell with it all" come screaming into your mind, STOP.

What would you say if it were your friend, sister or brother or son or daughter? You'd tell them not to. It's not worth it.

Drink will not be your crutch in your time of need – it's only as much use as a crutch made of ice in the Sahara desert!

WILL THE YEARNING EVER GO?

Take it from someone who knows: that yearning feeling never really disappears. Just like the yearning for a cigarette never fully goes. You get cravings. Not frequently, and sometimes you don't even notice them. That never changes. What changes is you. Your attitude changes. Your behaviour changes. Your ability to make choices. Your choice to rule your life instead of having it ruled for you.

Don't let your bad habits be masters of your life. You are the master of your life. You are in control.

Every time a yearning or a craving or a longing for a drink rears its ugly head with hedonistic promises of an evening of bliss free from worries and aches and pains, recognise it, look at it straight in the eye and decide:

DRINK, ILLNESS, FATIGUE, NO WILLPOWER

VS

HEALTHY, ALERT, PRODUCTIVE, LIVING YOUR DREAM

You may need to make this decision several times a night, and several times a week and several times a month, but eventually as time goes by, I promise you, these occasions of yearning or longing will diminish and become less frequent. Soon evenings will pass without you even giving a thought to drink. And soon you will have a yearning or a longing or a craving and think –"oh, yeah, my body wants a drink." Then you'll shrug it off and carry on with what you are doing – which is hopefully relaxing, productive and a step towards your goals of self-fulfilment.

These potential relapses are a danger to your happiness. Do not give in to them. If you are going through a crisis, there are plenty of other ways to seek help, which will actually help you. Alcohol will only fuel your depression, lack of self-worth and inability to cope.

Keep the faith: After a short while, you will yearn for exercise, great food, new voyages, friends and experiences... whatever takes your fancy.

You always have options:

Ask someone close to you for help.

Join a gym or dance/yoga/drama club.

Incorporate meditation as part of your daily routine.

Release your emotions through art: painting, writing, sculpting, needlework.

Spend time with your family, your pets, your friends.

If you are a believer, go to church.

If you did join the AA or something similar, go back to them.

Take up a new class.

Above all, deal with the problem at the root of your crisis. Much like when you gave up drinking in the first place, deal with the problem that triggers your sense of vulnerability and helplessness. Do not sidestep your problems by hitting the bottle. Empower yourself and tackle the problem or let go of trying to control situations if they are not within your control, as often that can be the source of many a frustration and reason for needing a drink.

You are not alone. You do not have to follow the orders of your weaker-willed ego. Follow the light of the stronger willed version of you. This version will shine and give you greater happiness and satisfaction in the long term.

You want to look back at your time of near relapse and/or crisis and say: "Thank you me. You saved me. I am still on track. Not only can I manage without drink, I can thrive and achieve." Instead of: "Oh no, here we go again. I can't help it. It's not my fault. God my head hurts. I haven't done anything on my project. I feel rotten. I really should spend time with the kids. I can't be bothered. It's not my fault. Gulp, gulp, gulp..." Down goes another £20 and another wasted evening which will be another wasted day the next day.... and your problems will still be there and your dreams and projects will still be gathering dust.

DO NOT RELAPSE. A crisis is not an excuse for giving up on your life. You owe it to yourself, that version of you that you have so enjoyed being, to carry on with that simple act of saying NO to drink and YES to life.

DO NOT USE YOUR EMOTIONAL CRISIS OR PROBLEMS AS AN EXCUSE TO START DRINKING AGAIN

You must keep drinking separate in your thoughts. All too often we are happy to fail because it seems so much easier. It seems so much easier just to give up instead of working away at our dreams and aspirations. But you are wrong and you know it. Remember how exhausting it was feeling like such a failure? The eternal worrying and eternal self-blame?

It is easier to not give up on yourself. It is easier to climb up the mountain of our dreams (albeit some days slower than others) and feel fulfilment as opposed to desperation or disappointment.

Negative feelings are much more draining on our emotions than positive feelings.

Do not use your sadness or laziness or lack of motivation, self-pity, loss of job - whatever the trigger may be - as an excuse to start drinking again.

A relapse doesn't have to be months or years after you have stopped. A relapse can also happen during the day or week you stop. Perhaps you are feeling gung-ho in the morning and by midday you're thinking : "To hell with this, I'm going to buy a bottle of wine, I need something to look forward to tonight."

STOP YOURSELF

Do not even stop to think. Go straight out for a jog, go into your meditation, run a bath, exercise, put on some music or go for a long walk. Anything to divert your mind.

Remember how good you felt when you didn't drink.

Remember the stinking hangover you'll feel.

Are 4 hours of drunken stupor a day really a fair or equal trade for missing out on a sustainable lifetime of happiness?

Put this on the scales of logic.

Put your life in balance.

Get things in perspective.

If you are unable to stop yourself and the side of you, the weaker-willed side of you, manages to convince you that you need a drink or that you deserve a drink, I can assure you that if you have properly "demonised' the habit of drinking you will regret this decision almost as soon as you have acted upon it. Definitely by the time the first sip of wine/drink passes your lips.

Two things will happen if you have "demonised" this bad habit properly:

1 - The wine/drink will taste bad to you. It will be sour in your mouth. It

will no longer be the nectar you once fooled yourself into thinking it was.

2 - Your body will physically reject it.

As you have spent weeks or months or even years purifying your body of this poison, your body will reject it as such. A poison. First through a bad taste and secondly, because your system is not used to it, the negative effects like stomach cramps will be amplified. Your headaches will be worse, your stomach aches will be more painful, your lack of focus will be worse.

Not only your body but also your mind will reject the drink. Your thoughts will be filled with remorse and regret. As you drink, your mind will remind you of all that you have enjoyed without drink. You will remind yourself of all the benefits you have enjoyed through having more focus and energy. If you carry on drinking in your moment of relapse you will be filled with regret and you will literally be forcing yourself to drink. Your weaker-willed self will be trying to convince you to carry on, get over the hump of feeling sick and feeling regret. If you just carry on it will get better.

Are you so convinced now that you have lived a more energetic and fulfilling life? Do you not see the next day stretching out in front of you filled with nothing but physical ailments, no energy or motivation? Your projects and dreams left to the wayside because you cannot focus thanks to your pounding headache?

Stop.

Just because you have relapsed and have bought the drink or have been given the drink, does not mean that you have to finish it. Listen to the sound part of your mind that is telling you it is a bad idea.

Remember that you have stopped to have a better life. Remember the sad and depressed life you had when you were dependent on drink. Do you really want to go back there? It is easier to achieve, to be happy to feel good about yourself.

Final Thoughts

SCARE YOURSELF

Every time you take a sip say: "Throat cancer"; make yourself look at images of throat cancer or cancer of the liver – do you really want to risk that?

Do you want to leave your children all alone to grow up without you?

It's a proven technique. That's why all our tobacco products now look more like clips from horror movies.

Give it a try.

ROUTINE/HABIT

If a change in your life is possible or there is an opportunity to change your life/job/location, then seize it, otherwise make the change yourself. Habits are made from routine.

Recognise when your hardest moments will be before they happen and circumvent them, put a new habit or a new routine in place before the impulse or craving can set in. Plan for your failure in order to avoid it.

This isn't avoiding the problem, this is making it easier for you to redirect your routine. Habit is routine and drinking is part of your routine. You'd be surprised how easy it would be to give up by just uprooting your life, moving somewhere new, doing different things and keeping busy.

You wouldn't even give drinking a second thought. But not all of us have the luxury of simply moving or relocating every time we get into a routine of bad habits, so we are going to change the routine in our current setting. This keeps us going in the long-term.

FIND SOMETHING YOU WANT MORE

If you fancy a drink in the evening when you get back from work, go straight into something else when or before you get back home:

Suggestions:

Go to the gym for half an hour before you get home, have a massage, sauna, swim, workout whatever is your preference. (Don't worry about the money, you'll be saving at least £10 a day on drink = £3,650 a year. I'm sure that will cover membership fees and spas treatments.

If you need to get back for the children, do something different at home so you physically cannot drink: Soak in a bath for half an hour. Get a bike/treadmill/rowing machine and do that or play outside with your children – trampoline, pogo stick or go on a bike ride with them.

Move away from the instinct of grabbing the bottle as soon as you get home. Unwind in a different way.

If none of the above appeals. Take 5 to 10 minutes to look at yourself in the mirror and repeat the following: "I do not want to drink. Drink is ruining my life. Drink is ruining the lives of my children. Drink is ruining my marriage. I want to stop. I want to feel better. I want to be better. I want to be happier. I want to be in control of my own life."

GETTING OVER THE HUMP.

When the yearning comes, take some long deep breaths. Focus on your intent (I suppose it is a kind of meditation), think only of not drinking, visualise the positive version of you that you want to be. When the moment passes, carry on with the cooking or playing or whatever you were doing. When the next pang comes. Stop do it again. Take yourself away and talk yourself and breathe your way out of the yearning or craving. Mix this with burning a little oil (uplifting essential oils, or peppermint to clear your mind) and you will feel different, stronger and more determined.

Take each step, each brick at a time.

SUMMARY

Drinking is not an evil.

Like all things, when done in moderation it can be enjoyed. You need to own your habit and demonise your habit because you have let it take over your life. If you can drink just once and a while and not so that you get completely off your head or completely inebriated, it can be something that you enjoy.

Abstention does not have to last forever.

Once you have conquered your dependency you can enjoy the odd drink here and there – if you want to and feel that you can. When it takes over your life, that is when it has to be stopped and eradicated like a poisonous root.

Your roots need to be healthy to feed you in a healthy sustainable way. Poisonous roots will poison your being.

In all honesty, once you have broken this bad habit, you will not want it any more.

The benefits far outweigh any false promises you thought alcohol could give you.

Life is all about choices. You may not have chosen the reason or excuse for *why* you became dependent on alcohol, but you can be in charge of making the choice to stop. To reclaim your life. To be the one in charge of your mind and your body.

Life is far too short to be poured down the drain. Don't wait for the perfect time. Just stop now. Don't wait until tomorrow.

Take steps to change your routine. Take steps to eradicate the bad influences in your life. Take steps to resolve your issues. Drink will not solve your problems or issues. It will simply rot your body and mind when drunk in excess.

OWN IT – HATE IT – BEAT IT

Fill your life and mind, not your glass and toilet.

Make today yesterday's tomorrow.

TODAY IS YESTERDAY'S TOMORRROW

this morning what was different because:

your legs and hands aren't swollen

your throat isn't sore

your mouth doesn't taste foul

your head doesn't hurt

you have more money in your pocket

your heart isn't beating erratically

you didn't smoke

you didn't do something stupid

you can remember last night

your skin is not dehydrated

you don't have stained mouth and teeth

you don't have to go to work with hangover breath

you have more energy

when you have breakfast you don't want to snooze

you are more focused

you didn't take in all those extra calories

you are happier

you are proud of yourself

you made the right choice – well done!

ABOUT THE AUTHOR

Francesca Hepton was born in Hawaii; she studied and worked for most of her life in Europe and currently resides in the quintessentially English town of Harrogate. She gained an MA Hons in Modern Languages from the University of St. Andrews, an Erasmus Diploma from the University of Toulouse. Her current passion is natural healing, she is a yoga practitioner and qualified crystal and Reiki healer, a successful writer and illustrator of children's books aimed increasing a positive self-image, self-awareness and self-confidence among youngsters.

Due to the personal circumstances in her life and driven by her love for her two sons, she decided to share her methods for effectively changing her life by writing the How to… series of books.

She is a firm believer in the pursuit of happiness and helping people fulfil their desires to be happy and succeed.

She is also founder of the "How To" think-tank team whose research focuses on the topics of self-belief, increased self-esteem and self-furtherment through:

"Egolosophy©" – the study of the self to be happier, focused and healthy
"Rejuvelaxation©" – a youthful approach through relaxation and positivity
"Yogitivity©" – inclusion of yoga to increase productivity and creativity

Believe you will succeed and you will

Printed in Great Britain
by Amazon

68070286R00058